lunchbox

lunches for work and school

THE AUSTRALIAN
Women's Weekly

contents

AUSTRALIAN CUP AND
SPOON MEASUREMENTS
ARE METRIC.
A CONVERSION CHART
APPEARS ON PAGE 77.

We're all saving harder these days, and one of the easiest ways is to take your lunch to work (or school). Buying lunch, and the necessary coffee to get you through the day, can add up to quite a lot during the year. This book has a variety of easy-to-make, tasty and healthy lunches that are suitable for children and adults, and healthy for the hip pocket.

Pamela Clark

Food Director

lunchbox essentials

Why settle for the same soggy sandwiches, overripe fruit and boring snacks in your lunchbox day after day? When making a packed lunch (either for a child or yourself) it is all about clever tricks to keep it interesting, healthy and appealing. A balanced lunch is key to remaining alert and active throughout the afternoon (whether at school or at work). There are various components that should always be included in a lunchbox – lean protein, dairy, healthy carbohydrates and fresh fruit and vegies. This checklist, however, does not mean variety and creativity need be sacrificed.

KIDS' LUNCHBOXES

It is important to consider where your child's lunch will be kept during the morning. If their lunch is in a warm place, bacteria will grow rapidly in the food and may cause food poisoning. Meat and dairy products are particularly prone to this. Cheese may turn slimy and soft in a hot lunchbox, and warm milk or warm yogurt is certainly not popular with kids. Salads wilt in the heat and tomato or cucumber in a warm sandwich is sure to make the bread soggy. So, if the school bag is going to be in the sun, putting an icepack in the lunchbox can usually keep the food cold until lunchtime, which keeps the food fresher and slows down the growth of bacteria. Freezing a drink and putting it in the lunchbox works too and provides a nice cool drink at lunchtime.

Fresh fruit is nature's 'no preparation required', individually packaged snack food, high in fibre, vitamins and minerals and ideal for the lunchbox. Foods that can be prepared either the night before or even on the weekend, and then frozen or refrigerated, are ideal for busy parents.

THE HEALTHY LUNCHBOX

Eating a variety of fresh food during the day means you're on your way to reaching the daily target of five servings of vegetables and two of fruit. Low GI carbohydrates such as wholemeal bread, grainy crispbread, rice and pasta, provide a slow release of energy so you can concentrate throughout the afternoon. Good sources of protein, such as tuna, eggs, chicken and ham, satisfy hunger and will keep you feeling fuller for longer.

PLAN & PREPARE

When doing the weekly grocery shop, make lunch ingredients a priority, not an afterthought. Indulge in your favourite meats, cheeses and breads and you won't feel like you are missing out by bringing lunch from home.

By planning and packing your lunches the night before, you will also find yourself naturally making healthier choices. It is much harder to resist fast food options if you're hungry and need to grab something quickly.

Lunch can be more than last night's leftovers, though curries, pastas, stir-fries and salads make excellent lunches. Cook large batches of pastas, curries, soups and stews and freeze them in single portions. Take your lunch out of the freezer the night before and defrost it in the fridge. Refrigerate it when you get to work, and at lunchtime it can be heated in the microwave.

The recipes in the 'lunches for kids' chapter use no nuts or nut oils to keep kids safe while at school.

STORAGE

Storing food so it travels well is important when preparing a packed lunch. There are many lunchbox options to keep food hot, cold and prevent messy leaks and spills.

Invest in good-quality food containers in different sizes. Use these to cut down on your use of plastic wrap and foil, which is costly and bad for the environment. At work it is always preferable to reheat food in a dish rather than in the container you have used to transport it in.

Fruit yogurts also can be frozen overnight to prevent bacteria growth and keep the rest of your lunch cool. Many fruits – grapes, watermelon, oranges, bananas and strawberries – can be frozen too.

lunches for kids

CORN, ZUCCHINI AND CHICKPEA FRITTERS

prep + cook time 30 minutes **makes** 14
nutritional count per fritter 3.3g total fat (1.5g saturated fat); 401kJ (96 cal);
10.3g carbohydrate; 5.1g protein; 2.4g fibre

400g (12½ ounces) canned chickpeas
  (garbanzo beans), rinsed, drained
¾ cup (110g) wholemeal self-raising flour
½ cup (125ml) milk
2 eggs
2 green onions (scallions), sliced thinly
1 large zucchini (150g), grated coarsely
310g (10 ounces) canned corn kernels,
  rinsed, drained
½ cup (60g) coarsely grated cheddar cheese
2 tablespoons coarsely chopped fresh
  mint leaves

1 Blend or process chickpeas until
chopped coarsely.
2 Sift flour into medium bowl; add any
husks from wheat to bowl. Make a well in
centre of flour; stir in combined milk and
eggs until smooth. Stir in chickpeas, onion,
zucchini, corn, cheese and mint; season.
3 Drop ¼ cup batter for each fritter, in
batches, into heated oiled large frying pan
(allow room for mixture to spread). Cook,
over medium heat, about 5 minutes or until
fritters are browned lightly both sides and
cooked through.

serving suggestion Tomato chutney or
yogurt for dipping.

TOMATO CHUTNEY AND BACON MUFFINS

prep + cook time 40 minutes (+ standing)   **makes** 18
nutritional count per muffin 4.5g total fat (2.5g saturated fat); 358kJ (85 cal);
8g carbohydrate; 3.1g protein; 0.5g fibre

¼ cup (40g) polenta
¼ cup (60ml) milk
2 rindless bacon slices (160g), chopped finely
2 green onions (scallions), sliced thinly
¾ cup (110g) self-raising flour
¼ cup (80g) tomato chutney
¼ cup (30g) coarsely grated cheddar cheese
60g (2 ounces) butter, melted
1 egg, lightly beaten
5 cherry tomatoes (100g)

1 Preheat oven to 180°C/350°F. Oil 18 holes of two 12-hole (1-tablespoon/20ml) mini muffin pans.
2 Combine polenta and milk in small bowl; cover, stand 20 minutes.
3 Cook bacon, stirring, in heated small frying pan, 2 minutes. Add onion to pan; cook, stirring, a further 2 minutes. Remove pan from heat; cool 5 minutes.
4 Sift flour into medium bowl; stir in chutney, cheese and the bacon mixture. Add melted butter, egg and polenta mixture; season. Mix until just combined. Divide mixture between pan holes. Cut tomatoes into quarters; top each muffin with a tomato quarter.
5 Bake muffins about 15 minutes. Stand muffins in pan 5 minutes before turning, top-side up, onto wire rack to cool.

ASPARAGUS AND TOMATO FRITTATA

prep + cook time 40 minutes **serves** 8
nutritional count per serving 8.7g total fat (3.8g saturated fat); 521kJ (124 cal);
1.4g carbohydrate; 10.1g protein; 0.6g fibre

8 eggs
¼ cup (60ml) milk
⅓ cup (40g) coarsely grated cheddar cheese
¼ cup small fresh basil leaves
100g (3 ounces) firm fresh ricotta cheese
170g (5½ ounces) asparagus, trimmed
200g (6½ ounces) mini roma tomatoes, halved

1 Preheat oven to 220°C/425°F.
2 Whisk eggs, milk and cheese in large jug; season.
3 Heat oiled 17cm (6¾-inch) (base measurement) ovenproof frying pan over medium heat. Add egg mixture to pan; cook, about 3 minutes, scraping edges of egg into centre of pan. Top with basil, ricotta, asparagus and tomatoes. Cook frittata, over medium heat, about 2 minutes or until base and edges are almost set. Transfer pan to oven; bake frittata, uncovered, about 15 minutes or until set and browned lightly. Stand 5 minutes.
4 Slide frittata onto serving plate; cut into eight pieces.

notes If necessary, protect the handle of the pan by wrapping it in a layer of foil. The frittata can be eaten hot, warm or at room temperature.

BACON AND HERB CHICKEN PATTIES

prep + cook time 25 minutes (+ refrigeration) **makes** 8
nutritional count per pattie 11.5g total fat (3.8g saturated fat); 1047kJ (250 cal);
9.6g carbohydrate; 26.6g protein; 0.8g fibre

1 clove garlic, crushed
2 green onions (scallions), chopped finely
500g (1 pound) minced (ground) chicken
1 egg
¾ cup (50g) stale wholemeal breadcrumbs
2 tablespoons finely chopped fresh
    flat-leaf parsley
2 tablespoons finely chopped fresh basil
⅓ cup (110g) tomato chutney
8 rindless bacon slices (500g)

1 Combine garlic, onion, chicken, egg, breadcrumbs, herbs and chutney in large bowl; season well. Shape mixture into eight patties.
2 Wrap each patty with one slice of bacon; place patties on tray. Cover, refrigerate 30 minutes.
3 Cook patties over medium heat in heated oiled large frying pan until browned on both sides and cooked through.

notes Freeze individual cooled patties in airtight containers for up to 1 month. Thaw overnight in the fridge; reheat in microwave at work or eat at room temperature, if taking to school. Make it a pattie roll by spreading a bread roll (or a pitta pocket or wrap) with tomato chutney and adding a sliced pattie and some salad.

CHICKEN AND ZUCCHINI CAKES

prep + cook time 50 minutes **makes** 12
nutritional count per cake 16.6g total fat (5.6g saturated fat); 1186kJ (284 cal);
15.3g carbohydrate; 17.5g protein; 1.8g fibre

7 eggs
1½ cups (225g) self-raising flour
1½ cups (180g) grated cheddar cheese
⅓ cup (80ml) olive oil
¼ cup each finely chopped fresh flat-leaf
  parsley and mint leaves
1 large brown onion (200g), chopped finely
4 medium zucchini (500g), grated coarsely
300g (9½ ounces) barbecued chicken,
  chopped finely
6 baby grape tomatoes (25g), halved

1 Preheat oven to 200°C/400°F. Line two
6-hole (¾-cup/180ml) texas muffin pans
with muffin wraps or paper cases.
2 Whisk eggs in large bowl; add sifted flour,
cheese, oil and herbs, mix well. Add onion,
zucchini and chicken; mix well. Season.
Spoon ½ cup mixture into muffin wraps;
top with tomato.
3 Bake cakes about 30 minutes. Stand in
pan 5 minutes before turning, top-side up,
onto a wire rack to cool.

notes Cool cakes before packing in airtight
containers; cakes will keep, refrigerated, for
up to 2 days. Cakes can also be frozen.
Pack a frozen cake in the lunchbox in the
morning and it will be thawed by lunchtime.

CHICKEN AND KUMARA SANDWICHES

prep + cook time 35 minutes (+ cooling) **makes** 3
nutritional count per sandwich 18.8g total fat (8.2g saturated fat); 2097kJ (501 cal);
31.6g carbohydrate; 27.5g protein; 8g fibre

1 medium kumara (orange sweet potato)
   (400g), sliced thinly
1 cup (160g) shredded barbecued chicken
2 tablespoons soft ricotta cheese
1 tablespoon mayonnaise
2 teaspoons finely chopped fresh
   flat-leaf parsley
6 slices wholemeal bread (270g)
30g (1 ounce) butter, softened
20g (¾ ounce) baby spinach leaves

1 Preheat oven to 200°C/400°F. Oil oven tray.
2 Place kumara, in single layer, on oven tray; spray with cooking oil. Season. Roast about 15 minutes or until tender. Cool.
3 Meanwhile, combine chicken, ricotta, mayonnaise and parsley in medium bowl; season to taste.
4 Spread bread with butter; sandwich spinach, kumara and chicken mixture between bread slices. Cut the sandwiches however you like.

HAM, CORN AND CHEESE SANDWICHES

prep time 15 minutes **makes** 3
nutritional count per sandwich 20.2g total fat (11.3g saturated fat); 2069kJ (494 cal);
53g carbohydrate; 21.9g protein; 6.6g fibre

1 small carrot (70g), grated coarsely
125g (4 ounces) canned creamed corn
1 tablespoon finely chopped fresh chives
6 slices sourdough bread (300g)
30g (1 ounce) butter, softened
3 slices (70g) cheddar cheese
100g (3 ounces) shaved leg ham

1 Combine carrot, corn and chives in medium bowl; season to taste.
2 Spread bread with butter; sandwich corn mixture, cheese and ham between bread slices. Cut sandwiches in half.

note You can use any type of sliced bread.

CREAMY SALMON, SPINACH AND AVOCADO SANDWICHES

prep + cook time 15 minutes **makes** 3
nutritional count per sandwich 29.9g total fat (10g saturated fat); 2222kJ (531 cal); 39.6g carbohydrate; 22.8g protein; 6.3g fibre

250g (8 ounces) canned salmon slices
¼ cup (75g) mayonnaise
½ small avocado (100g), sliced thinly
1 tablespoon lemon juice
6 slices wholemeal bread (270g)
30g (1 ounce) butter, softened
20g (¾ ounce) baby spinach leaves

1 Drain and flake salmon; combine in small bowl with mayonnaise.
2 Place avocado and juice in small bowl; toss to coat, drain.
3 Spread bread with butter; sandwich salmon mixture, avocado and spinach between bread slices. Season to taste. Cut sandwiches however you like.

MARBLED LAMINGTONS

prep + cook time 1¼ hours (+ cooling & standing) **makes** 25
nutritional count per lamington 10.2g total fat (7.1g saturated fat); 864kJ (206 cal);
27.4g carbohydrate; 2.2g protein; 1.1g fibre

125g (4 ounces) butter, softened
1 cup (220g) caster (superfine) sugar
1 teaspoon vanilla extract
3 eggs
1¾ cups (260g) self-raising flour
½ cup (125ml) milk
2 tablespoons cocoa powder
2 cups (160g) desiccated coconut
chocolate icing
15g (½ ounce) butter, chopped
4 cups (640g) icing (confectioners') sugar
½ cup (50g) cocoa powder
¾ cup (180ml) milk

1 Preheat oven to 180°C/350°F. Grease
23cm (9½-inch) square cake pan; line base
and sides with baking paper, extending
paper 5cm (2-inches) over long sides.
2 Beat butter, sugar and extract in small
bowl with electric mixer until light and fluffy.
Beat in eggs, one at a time.
3 Stir in sifted flour and milk, in two batches.
Spoon half the mixture into medium bowl;
stir in sifted cocoa (leave remaining mixture
plain). Spoon mixtures alternately into pan;
using skewer, gently swirl mixtures together
to create a marbled effect.

4 Bake cake about 35 minutes. Stand cake
in pan 10 minutes before turning, top-side
up, onto baking-paper-covered wire rack
to cool.
5 Make chocolate icing.
6 Cut cake into 25 squares; dip each square
into chocolate icing, drain off excess. Toss
squares in coconut. Place lamingtons on
wire rack to set.
chocolate icing Melt butter in medium
heatproof bowl over medium saucepan of
simmering water. Sift icing sugar and cocoa
into melted butter; stir in milk. Stir until icing
is of a coating consistency.

notes To keep the coconut free of chocolate
drips, spread out half the coconut in a tray
and coat half the lamingtons before using
the remaining coconut for the remaining
lamingtons. This gives the lamingtons a
clean look. Lamingtons can be frozen for
up to 3 months.

PASSIONFRUIT YOGURT CUPCAKES

prep + cook time 50 minutes (+ cooling) **makes** 12
nutritional count per cupcake 12.7g total fat (7.9g saturated fat); 879kJ (210 cal);
19.8g carbohydrate; 3.8g protein; 1.9g fibre

90g (3 ounces) unsalted butter, softened
½ cup (110g) caster (superfine) sugar
1 teaspoon finely grated orange rind
2 eggs
1 cup (150g) self-raising flour
½ cup (125ml) passionfruit pulp
⅓ cup (95g) greek-style yogurt
cream cheese icing
30g (1 ounce) unsalted butter, softened
100g (3 ounces) cream cheese, at
    room temperature
1 teaspoon finely grated orange rind
1½ cups (240g) icing (confectioners') sugar

1 Preheat oven to 180°C/350°F. Line
12-hole (¹/₃-cup/80ml) muffin pan with
paper cases.
2 Beat butter, sugar, rind and eggs in small
bowl with electric mixer until light and fluffy.
3 Stir in sifted flour, passionfruit and yogurt.
Divide mixture evenly into paper cases;
smooth surface.
4 Bake cakes about 25 minutes. Stand
cakes in pan 5 minutes before turning,
top-side up, onto wire rack to cool.
5 Make cream cheese icing. Spread cold
cakes with icing.
cream cheese icing Beat butter, cream
cheese and rind in small bowl with electric
mixer until light and fluffy; gradually beat in
sifted icing sugar.

notes Uniced cakes can be frozen for up to
3 months. Top with extra passionfruit pulp
and serve as an after-school treat, or stir
the pulp through the icing before using to
ice the cakes. We used the pulp of two large
passionfruit (about 2 tablespoons).

DOUBLE-CHOC COCONUT COOKIES

prep + cook time 40 minutes (+ cooling) **makes** about 25
nutritional count per cookie 7.2g total fat (4.8g saturated fat); 505kJ (121 cal);
12.6g carbohydrate; 1.5g protein; 1.2g fibre

125g (4 ounces) butter, softened
¾ cup (165g) firmly packed light brown sugar
1 egg
1 cup (160g) wholemeal self-raising flour
1 cup (80g) desiccated coconut
⅓ cup (35g) Milo
⅓ cup (65g) milk choc Bits

1 Preheat oven to 180°C/350°F. Line oven trays with baking paper.
2 Beat butter, sugar and egg in small bowl with electric mixer until light and fluffy. Stir in sifted flour (and any husks in the sifter), coconut, Milo and choc Bits.
3 Roll level tablespoons of mixture into balls. Place about 5cm (2 inches) apart on trays, flatten slightly. Bake about 15 minutes; cool on trays.

note Store cookies in a glass jar or airtight container for up to 1 week or freeze for up to 3 months.

WHEATY BANANA MUFFINS

prep + cook time 45 minutes (+ cooling) **makes** 12
nutritional count per muffin 5.9g total fat (3.7g saturated fat); 1025kJ (245 cal);
43.5g carbohydrate; 4.1g protein; 2.4g fibre

1 medium banana (200g)
1 tablespoon lemon juice
1½ cups (225g) self-raising flour
½ cup (110g) firmly packed light brown sugar
1 cup (100g) crushed Weet-Bix
1 cup (280g) mashed banana
½ cup (125ml) buttermilk
80g (2½ ounces) butter, melted
1 egg, beaten lightly
honey icing
1 tablespoon honey
2 teaspoons milk
½ cup (80g) icing (confectioners') sugar

1 Preheat oven to 180°C/350°F. Line a 12-hole (⅓-cup/80ml) muffin pan with paper cases.
2 Thickly slice banana; combine with juice in medium bowl.
3 Sift flour and sugar into large bowl; stir in Weet-Bix and mashed banana. Add buttermilk, butter and egg; stir only until mixture is just combined. Divide mixture between paper cases; top with banana slices.
4 Bake about 25 minutes. Stand muffins in pan 5 minutes before turning, top-side up, onto wire rack to cool.
5 Make honey icing. Spoon icing over cold muffins; stand until set.
honey icing Combine honey and milk in small saucepan; stir over low heat until combined. Remove from heat; gradually stir in sifted icing sugar.

notes You will need 2 large (460g) overripe bananas to make 1 cup mashed banana. Uniced muffins can be frozen for up to 3 months.

sandwiches and wraps

PORK BAHN MI

prep time 10 minutes **makes** 2
nutritional count per roll 11.4g total fat (3g saturated fat); 1495kJ (357 cal);
34.2g carbohydrate; 26.9g protein; 3.5g fibre

1 lebanese cucumber (130g)
1 green onion (scallion)
2 long white rolls (120g)
2 tablespoons japanese mayonnaise
6 slices roast pork (150g)
½ small carrot (35g), grated coarsely
1 long fresh red chilli, sliced thinly (optional)
4 sprigs fresh coriander
1 tablespoon soy sauce

1 Use a vegetable peeler to cut the cucumber into ribbons. Cut onion the same length as the bread rolls.
2 Cut rolls lengthways, through the top, without cutting all the way through. Spread rolls with mayonnaise; layer pork, cucumber, onion, carrot, chilli and coriander into rolls. Sprinkle over sauce when ready for lunch.

notes Barbecued chicken can be used in place of the pork.
Wrap roll in baking paper. Pack soy sauce in small airtight container. Keep rolls in fridge until about ½ hour before ready to serve. Sprinkle over sauce when ready for lunch.

FELAFEL AND CABBAGE SALAD POCKETS

prep time 25 minutes **makes** 2
nutritional count per pitta 35.7g total fat (5.6g saturated fat); 3087kJ (737 cal);
72.7g carbohydrate; 22g protein; 16.2g fibre

½ large tomato (110g)
2 tablespoons fresh flat-leaf parsley leaves
½ small lebanese cucumber (65g)
1 large green onion (scallion)
1 cup (80g) shredded red cabbage
1 tablespoon olive oil
1 tablespoon lemon juice
6 mini felafel (180g)
2 small pocket pitta breads (170g)
½ cup (120g) baba ghanoush
8 drained fefferoni peppers, optional

1 Coarsely chop tomato, parsley, cucumber and onion. Combine tomato, parsley, cucumber, onion, cabbage and combined oil and juice in medium bowl; season to taste. Pack in small airtight container until ready to serve.

2 At work, microwave felafel about 1 minute on high (100%) or until heated through. Break felafel up with a fork. Cut pockets in half. Spread inside of pitta with baba ghanoush; add felafel, cabbage salad and peppers.

notes You can use prepared tabbouleh instead of the cabbage salad, if you prefer. If no microwave is available at work, spread the pitta with baba ghanoush, fill with felafel and wrap securely in foil before leaving home. Pack a spoon to add the salad just before serving.

MOROCCAN TUNA WRAP

prep + cook time 10 minutes **serves** 1
nutritional count per serving 28.9g total fat (6.7g saturated fat); 2231kJ (533 cal);
25.8g carbohydrate; 30.5g protein; 4.4g fibre

1½ tablespoons slivered almonds
½ wedge preserved lemon
¼ small red onion (25g), chopped finely
1 small clove garlic, crushed
95g (3-ounces) canned tuna in olive oil,
   drained
1 tablespoon finely chopped fresh coriander
   leaves (cilantro)
1½ tablespoons low-fat mayonnaise
¼ teaspoon ras el hanout
20g (¾ ounce) fetta cheese, crumbled
1 large bread wrap (50g)
½ medium egg (plum) tomato (40g),
   sliced thickly
20g (¾ ounce) rocket (arugula) leaves

1 Roast nuts in small dry frying pan over medium-high heat until browned lightly. Remove from pan; cool.
2 Discard flesh from preserved lemon, wash and dry rind; chop rind finely.
3 Place lemon, onion, garlic, tuna, coriander, mayonnaise, ras el hanout, cheese and nuts in medium bowl. Use a fork to mash until combined. Season to taste.
4 At work, place tuna mixture in centre of wrap, top with tomato and rocket. Roll up firmly to secure filling.

notes Ras el hanout is a Moroccan spice mix found in specialty spice shops and some delicatessens.
Pack tuna mixture, tomato and rocket in separate containers and assemble at work.

BEEF ROLLS WITH CELERIAC REMOULADE

prep + cook time 10 minutes **makes** 2
nutritional count per roll 24.2g total fat (5.2g saturated fat); 4248kJ (1014 cal);
148.3g carbohydrate; 43g protein; 12.4g fibre

2 cloves garlic, peeled
2 teaspoons mustard seeds
4 cornichons (25g), chopped finely
60g (2 ounces) peeled celeriac (celery root),
    grated coarsely
¼ cup coarsely chopped fresh flat-leaf parsley
½ cup (150g) low-fat mayonnaise
1 tablespoon dijon mustard
½ teaspoon lemon juice
2 small rye french bread sticks (480g)
150g (4½ ounces) thinly sliced rare roast beef

1 Place garlic in small saucepan, cover with cold water; bring to the boil, drain.
2 Meanwhile, place mustard seeds in small dry frying pan; cook over medium heat until seeds begin to pop.
3 Crush garlic into medium bowl. Add seeds, cornichons, celeriac, parsley, mayonnaise, mustard and juice; mix well. Season to taste.
4 Split bread sticks in half through the top, without cutting all the way through; fill with beef and remoulade. Wrap roll securely in baking paper or lunch wrap.

notes If you don't have any leftover roast beef, buy thinly sliced cold roast beef from the delicatessen. You could replace the beef with barbecued chicken. You need about a quarter of an average celeriac. Celeriac discolours quickly once cut, so use it straight away or place in a bowl of cold water with lemon juice added.

CHUNKY HAM AND FIG SANDWICHES

prep + cook time 15 minutes **makes** 2
nutritional count per sandwich 30.9g total fat (15.9g saturated fat); 2991kJ (715 cal);
65.7g carbohydrate; 39.1g protein; 8.6g fibre

1½ tablespoons low-fat mayonnaise
2 teaspoons dijon mustard
4 slices soy and linseed bread (280g)
2 medium figs (120g), sliced thinly
160g (5 ounces) sliced leg ham off the bone
⅔ cup (80g) coarsely grated cheddar cheese
20g (¾ ounce) butter, softened
20g (¾ ounce) watercress, optional

1 Combine mayonnaise and mustard in small bowl.
2 Spread mayonnaise mixture on one slice of bread, top with fig, ham and cheese. Top with remaining bread slice. Wrap tightly in plastic wrap.
3 Just before serving, butter outside of bread; toast sandwich in heated sandwich press. Serve with watercress, if you like.

notes Many office kitchens have a sandwich press. If not, you could toast the sandwich at home then reheat it gently in the microwave at lunchtime, although it will not be as crisp. Pack the butter in a small airtight container. The sandwich is also delicious untoasted. Spread bread with a little fig jam when fresh figs are unavailable.

PEA, BROAD BEAN AND EGG ROLL UPS

prep + cook time 25 minutes **makes** 2
nutritional count per roll 10.8g total fat (4.3g saturated fat); 1144kJ (273 cal);
20g carbohydrate; 19.7g protein; 8.2g fibre

2 eggs
1 cup (140g) frozen broad beans (fava beans)
10g (½ ounce) butter
1 shallot (25g), chopped finely
½ cup (60g) frozen peas
1 tablespoon finely grated lemon rind
⅓ cup (25g) finely grated parmesan cheese
1 teaspoon chopped fresh mint leaves
2 large bread wraps (50g)

1 Place eggs in small saucepan of cold water; bring to the boil. Boil, uncovered, 3 minutes; drain. Place eggs under cold water until cool enough to handle; peel eggs.
2 Meanwhile, boil, steam or microwave broad beans for 1 minute or until thawed. Rinse under cold water; when cool enough to handle, peel beans.
3 Heat butter in medium frypan over medium heat; cook shallot, stirring, until soft. Add broad beans, peas and rind; cook, stirring, until peas and beans are bright green. Add cheese, stir to combine.
4 Transfer pea mixture to medium bowl; mash coarsely with a fork. Add mint and eggs; mash coarsely. Season to taste.
5 Spoon mixture into centre of wrap, roll up firmly; secure with folded baking paper.

note Cut wraps in half, if you like.

CHICKEN AND BEAN BURRITOS

prep + cook time 25 minutes **makes** 4
nutritional count per burrito 22.4g total fat (7.2g saturated fat); 1900kJ (454 cal);
33g carbohydrate; 27.5g protein; 4.3g fibre

1 medium lime (90g)
¼ medium red onion (40g), chopped finely
1 fresh long green chilli, chopped finely
½ medium tomato (75g), chopped coarsely
½ cup lightly packed fresh coriander leaves
   (cilantro), chopped coarsely
½ cup (100g) rinsed, drained canned
   red kidney beans
½ cup (60g) coarsely grated cheddar cheese
1 cup (150g) cooked white long-grain rice
1 medium ripe avocado (250g)
4 x 22cm (8¾-inch) burrito tortillas
1½ cups (240g) shredded barbecued chicken

1 Finely grate 1 teaspoon of rind from lime; squeeze 2 tablespoons juice from lime.
2 Combine onion, chilli, tomato, coriander, rind, beans and cheese in large bowl.
3 Microwave rice about 30 seconds on high (100%) or until heated through. Add to bowl with half the juice; season to taste.
4 Peel avocado; mash in small bowl with remaining juice, season to taste.
5 Place tortillas on sheets of baking paper. Spread a quarter of the avocado onto each tortilla; top with chicken and rice mixture. Roll firmly to enclose filling; wrap in paper then foil.

notes For a vegetarian option, add extra beans in place of the chicken.
You need to cook ⅓ cup (65g) raw rice to get the amount of cooked rice used here. You could also use the microwave rice now available in most supermarkets.

salads

POACHED CHICKEN SOBA NOODLE SALAD

prep + cook time 30 minutes **serves** 4
nutritional count per serving 11.4g total fat (2.4g saturated fat); 1914kJ (457 cal);
54.6g carbohydrate; 30.2g protein; 4.2g fibre

1 litre (4 cups) boiling water
1 teaspoon sesame oil
2 chicken breast fillets (360g)
2 teaspoons sesame seeds
270g (8½ ounces) dried soba noodles
150g (4½ ounces) snow peas, trimmed
1½ tablespoons tahini
¼ cup (60ml) rice vinegar
1½ tablespoons soy sauce
1½ teaspoons caster (superfine) sugar
3 teaspoons mirin

1 Bring the water and half the oil to the boil in medium saucepan; add chicken, simmer gently, covered, about 10 minutes or until just cooked through. Cool chicken in liquid 10 minutes, then shred chicken. Discard cooking liquid.
2 Meanwhile, toast seeds in small dry frying pan over medium heat until browned lightly; remove from pan.
3 Cook noodles and snow peas in large saucepan of boiling water until just tender; drain. Rinse under cold water; drain. Slice snow peas thinly.
4 Combine tahini, vinegar, sauce, sugar, mirin and remaining sesame oil in medium bowl. Add noodles, snow peas and chicken; toss to coat. Sprinkle salad with sesame seeds to serve.

note Soba are fresh or dried Japanese noodles made from buckwheat and wheat flour. They're available from Asian food stores and major supermarkets.

CHAR-GRILLED VEGETABLE, CHICKEN AND COUSCOUS SALAD

prep time 15 minutes **serves** 4
nutritional count per serving 17.8g total fat (4.8g saturated fat); 2328kJ (556 cal);
65g carbohydrate; 31g protein; 4.4g fibre

1½ cups (300g) couscous
1½ cups (375ml) boiling water
1 tablespoon olive oil
2 cups (420g) drained mixed char-grilled
   vegetables
1 cup each lightly packed fresh mint and
   flat-leaf parsley leaves
1½ cups (250g) shredded barbecued chicken
½ cup (140g) greek-style yogurt
1 medium lemon (140g), cut into wedges

1 Combine couscous, the water and oil in large heatproof bowl. Cover; stand 5 minutes or until liquid is absorbed. Fluff with fork. Season to taste.
2 Chop vegetables and herbs coarsely.
3 Add chicken, vegetables and herbs to couscous in large bowl; toss to combine. Serve with yogurt and lemon wedges.

notes This salad will keep for up to 2 days in the refrigerator. Pack yogurt and lemon wedges separately.
You need about half a barbecued chicken.
We used 2 x 280g jars of mixed char-grilled vegetables in oil (not the pickled variety); you can also buy marinated grilled vegetables from the delicatessen.

ROAST BEEF AND PANZANELLA SALAD

prep + cook time 20 minutes **serves** 2
nutritional count per serving 43.4g total fat (6.5g saturated fat); 2719kJ (650 cal);
40.6g carbohydrate; 19.6g protein; 6.5g fibre

150g (4½ ounces) ciabatta bread
⅓ cup (80ml) olive oil
1 clove garlic, crushed
2 tablespoons red wine vinegar
150g (4½ ounces) bottled roasted
    red capsicum (bell pepper)
½ cup lightly packed fresh basil leaves
170g (5½ ounces) red grape tomatoes, halved
⅓ cup (50g) seeded black olives
1 tablespoon rinsed, drained baby capers
100g (3 ounces) rare roast beef slices

1 Preheat oven to 200°C/400°F. Line oven
tray with baking paper.
2 Tear bread into bite-sized pieces. Place in
single layer on tray. Drizzle with half the oil.
Bake about 10 minutes or until golden.
3 To make dressing, place garlic, vinegar
and remaining oil in screw-top jar; shake
well. Season to taste.
4 Drain and coarsely chop capsicum. Tear
basil leaves in half.
5 Combine capsicum, basil, tomato, olives,
capers and bread in large bowl; top with
beef. Drizzle with dressing.

notes When taking to work, keep bread,
beef and dressing in separate containers.
Store in the fridge, and combine just before
you are ready for lunch.

QUINOA, CHICKEN AND PARSLEY SALAD

prep + cook time 20 minutes **serves** 4
nutritional count per serving 19.2g total fat (3.4g saturated fat); 1188kJ (284 cal);
7.4g carbohydrate; 19.2g protein; 1.8g fibre

½ cup (100g) quinoa
1 cup (250ml) water
⅓ cup (80ml) lemon juice
¼ cup (60ml) olive oil
250g (8 ounces) cherry tomatoes, halved
1 bunch each fresh flat-leaf parsley and mint, chopped coarsely
3 green onions (scallions), sliced thinly lengthways
1½ cups (250g) shredded barbecued chicken

1 Place quinoa and the water in small saucepan; bring to the boil. Reduce heat; simmer, covered, about 10 minutes or until water is absorbed and grains are tender. Remove from heat.
2 For dressing, combine juice and oil in large bowl; season to taste. Add quinoa, tomato, herbs, onion and chicken to dressing; toss to combine.

notes You need about half a barbecued chicken for this recipe. Package dressing separately. Store salad in fridge; combine with dressing just before serving.

PEA AND HAM BROWN RICE SALAD

prep + cook time 45 minutes (+ cooling) **serves** 4
nutritional count per serving 21.4g total fat (7.9g saturated fat); 1667kJ (401 cal);
29.3g carbohydrate; 20.7g protein; 3.8g fibre

1½ cups (300g) medium-grain brown rice
3 cups (750ml) water
1 cup (120g) frozen peas
2 tablespoons olive oil
1½ tablespoons red wine vinegar
1 large red capsicum (bell pepper) (350g),
    chopped finely
1 green onion (scallion), sliced thinly
100g (3 ounces) coarsely grated
    cheddar cheese
200g (6½ ounces) sliced ham,
    coarsely chopped

1 Place rice and the water in medium saucepan; bring to the boil. Reduce heat to low; simmer, covered, about 40 minutes or until water is absorbed and rice is tender. Spread rice in a thin layer on tray lined with baking paper; cool.

2 Meanwhile, cook peas in small saucepan of boiling water until just tender; drain. Rinse under cold water; drain.

3 For dressing, combine oil and vinegar in large bowl. Add rice, peas, capsicum, onion, cheese and ham to dressing; toss to combine. Season to taste.

notes This salad will keep for 2 days in the refrigerator. Try it with leftover roast chicken or turkey.
Keep salad refrigerated; bring to room temperature before serving.

TUNA AND BEAN SALAD

prep + cook time 15 minutes **serves** 4
nutritional count per serving 26.2g total fat (4g saturated fat); 1946kJ (465 cal);
21.4g carbohydrate; 31.4g protein; 10.6g fibre

250g (8 ounces) green beans, halved
   crossways
425g (13½ ounces) canned tuna in olive oil,
   drained
1 bunch fresh coriander (cilantro)
¼ cup (60ml) olive oil
2 tablespoons red wine vinegar
2 x 400g (12½ ounces) canned mixed beans,
   rinsed, drained
½ small red onion (50g), sliced thinly

1 Cook green beans in small saucepan of
boiling water until just tender, drain. Rinse
under cold water; drain.
2 Meanwhile, flake tuna into large chunks.
Coarsely chop coriander leaves and stems;
discard roots.
3 For dressing, combine oil and vinegar in
large bowl. Add all the beans, tuna, onion
and coriander to dressing; toss to combine.
Season to taste.

notes Keep refrigerated for up to 2 days;
bring to room temperature before serving.
Package dressing separately; combine just
before serving.

BEEF, BEETROOT AND POTATO SALAD

prep + cook time 25 minutes (+ cooling) **serves** 4
nutritional count per serving 6.3g total fat (3.3g saturated fat); 1283kJ (307 cal);
36.9g carbohydrate; 21.5g protein; 6g fibre

800g (1½ pounds) kipfler (fingerling) potatoes
425g (13½ ounces) canned baby beetroot
(beets)
¼ cup (60g) light sour cream
2 tablespoons lemon juice
3 teaspoons horseradish cream
3 teaspoons finely chopped fresh dill
120g (4 ounces) mesclun
225g (7 ounces) shaved rare roast beef

1 Scrub potatoes; cover with cold water in medium saucepan. Bring to the boil; reduce heat, simmer, covered, until tender. Drain potatoes; halve lengthways. Cool slightly.
2 Meanwhile, drain and halve beetroot.
3 To make dressing, combine sour cream, juice, horseradish cream and dill in small bowl. Season to taste.
4 Combine potato, beetroot, mesclun and beef in large bowl; drizzle over dressing.

notes Prepare this salad the night before; it is best dressed just before serving. Place beetroot in base of lunch container, top with mesclun, potato and beef; pack dressing separately. Store in the fridge; bring to room temperature before serving.

frittatas and pastries

FRITTATA PRIMAVERA

prep + cook time 40 minutes (+ cooling) **serves** 4
nutritional count per serving 33.1g total fat (17.9g saturated fat); 1737kJ (415 cal);
5g carbohydrate; 23.7g protein; 3.3g fibre

170g (5½ ounces) asparagus, trimmed,
    chopped coarsely
2 small zucchini (180g), sliced thinly
    lengthways
1 cup (120g) frozen peas
8 eggs
½ cup (125ml) pouring cream
½ cup lightly packed fresh mint leaves, torn
150g (4½ ounces) fetta cheese, crumbled

1 Preheat oven to 180°C/350°C. Oil 20cm x
30cm (8-inch x 12-inch) rectangular pan;
line base with baking paper, extending
paper 5cm (2 inches) over long sides.
2 Place asparagus, zucchini and peas into
small saucepan of boiling water. Return to
the boil; drain immediately, transfer to bowl
of iced water until cold. Drain well.
3 Whisk eggs and cream in large jug until
combined. Add mint; season.

4 Place cheese and vegetables in pan; pour
over egg mixture. Bake, uncovered, in oven,
about 25 minutes or until set.
5 Cool frittata before cutting into slices.

notes Store cooled frittata, covered, in
the refrigerator for up to 2 days. You can
also start cooking this frittata in a non-stick
frying pan on the stove top and finish it
under the grill (broiler).
The frittata can be eaten either warm or
at room temperature.

POTATO, OLIVE AND CAPSICUM FRITTATA

prep + cook time 30 minutes **serves** 4
nutritional count per serving 42.2g total fat (17.3g saturated fat); 2311kJ (552 cal);
19.6g carbohydrate; 22.7g protein; 3.3g fibre

1 cured chorizo sausage (170g)
500g (1 pound) desiree potatoes, cut into
 3cm (1¼-inch) cubes
1 tablespoon olive oil
8 eggs
½ cup (125ml) pouring cream
2 tablespoons finely chopped fresh
 flat-leaf parsley
½ cup (120g) drained char-grilled
 red capsicum (bell pepper), cut into strips
¼ cup (40g) seeded black olives

1 Thickly slice chorizo on the diagonal; place in 18cm (7¼-inch) (base measurement) ovenproof frying pan over high heat. Cook chorizo until crisp; remove from pan. Wipe pan clean with absorbent paper towel.
2 Meanwhile, boil, steam or microwave potato about 5 minutes or until potato is just tender; drain.
3 Heat oil in same frying pan; cook potato, stirring, over medium-high heat, until golden.
4 Meanwhile, whisk eggs and cream in large jug until combined. Stir in parsley; season.

5 Add chorizo, capsicum and olives to potato in pan. Pour egg mixture over ingredients in pan. Cook mixture, over low heat, about 6 minutes or until base and side of egg is set.
6 Meanwhile, preheat grill (broiler). Grill frittata about 5 minutes or until just set (see notes). Turn frittata onto large board; cut into wedges.

notes You need a frying pan with a heatproof handle for this recipe. If the handle is not heatproof, wrap it in two layers of foil. Grill the frittata about 15cm (6 inches) below the heat. Store the cooled frittata on a plate, covered with plastic wrap, in the fridge for up to 2 days. The frittata can be eaten either warm or at room temperature.

PEPPER, BEEF AND MUSHROOM PIES

prep + cook time 1¼ hours (+ cooling) **makes** 8
nutritional count per pie 34.5g total fat (17g saturated fat); 2489kJ (595 cal);
45.7g carbohydrate; 24.3g protein; 3.1g fibre

You need eight oval pie dishes with a top
measurement of 9cm x 11cm (3¾-inches
x 4½-inches), a base measurement of
6.5cm x 9.5cm (2¾-inches x 4-inches)
and a depth of 2.5cm (1-inch).

1 tablespoon olive oil
300g (9½ ounces) button mushrooms,
   chopped coarsely
1 medium brown onion (150g), chopped finely
600g (1¼ pounds) minced (ground) beef
2 tablespoons cornflour (cornstarch)
1½ cups (375ml) beef stock
2 tablespoons tomato paste
2 teaspoons freshly ground black pepper
3 sheets puff pastry
2 sheets shortcrust pastry
1 egg

1 Heat half the oil in large saucepan over
high heat. Cook mushrooms, stirring, until
well browned. Remove from pan.
2 Heat remaining oil over medium-high heat
in same pan. Cook onion, stirring, until soft.
Add beef, cook, stirring, over high heat until
beef is browned.
3 Blend cornflour and ¼ cup stock in small
bowl until smooth; stir in paste. Return
mushrooms to pan with cornflour mixture,
remaining stock and pepper. Bring to the
boil; simmer, uncovered, about 3 minutes
or until thickened. Cool completely.

4 Preheat oven to 200°C/400°F.
5 Turn pie dishes upside-down and cut out
eight 9cm x 11cm ovals from the puff pastry.
Refrigerate until required.
6 Cut both sheets of shortcrust pastry into
quarters to give eight squares. Roll squares
on lightly floured surface until large enough
to line the eight tins. Lightly oil tins; ease
pastry into tins, press into bases and sides,
trim edges. Cover pastry with baking paper;
fill with dried beans or rice. Place tins on
oven trays. Bake 10 minutes; remove beans
and paper. Bake pastry cases a further
5 minutes. Cool pastry cases completely.
7 Fill pastry cases with ½ cup cold beef
mixture. Brush edges of pastry with lightly
beaten egg. Top with puff pastry; press
edges to seal. Brush tops with a little more
egg. Cut steam holes in top of pies. Bake
about 30 minutes or until pastry is golden.

notes Cool pies before packing in airtight
containers; refrigerate for up to 2 days. Pies
can also be frozen cooked or uncooked.
Uncooked pies can be baked from frozen.
Thaw baked pies before reheating.
At work, you can warm the pies gently in a
toaster oven, or on low in the microwave,
however, the pastry won't be as crisp.

ARTICHOKE AND PROSCIUTTO TART

prep + cook time 1 hour **serves** 4
nutritional count per serving 72.5g total fat (38.4g saturated fat); 4621kJ (1104 cal); 84.6g carbohydrate; 27.6g protein; 5.4g fibre

4½ sheets shortcrust pastry
400g (12½ ounces) canned artichokes in brine, drained
50g (1½ ounces) prosciutto
4 eggs
⅓ cup (80ml) pouring cream
½ cup (60g) finely grated cheddar cheese
1 tablespoon basil leaves

1 Preheat oven to 200°C/400°F.
2 Overlap pastry sheets by 1cm (½-inch), pressing down firmly to join. Oil 12.5cm x 35cm (5-inch x 14-inch) loose-based rectangular flan tin. Ease pastry into tin, press into base and sides; trim edges. Place tin on oven tray. Cover pastry with baking paper; fill with dried beans or rice. Bake 10 minutes; remove beans and paper. Bake pastry case a further 15 minutes.
3 Meanwhile, cut artichokes into quarters. Tear prosciutto into bite-size pieces.
4 Whisk eggs, cream and cheese in large jug; season.
5 Pour egg mixture into pastry case; top with artichokes, cut-side up, and prosciutto. Bake about 25 minutes or until filling sets. Serve sprinkled with basil.

notes Cool tart before cutting into eight slices. Refrigerate, in an airtight container, for up to 2 days. Tart can also be frozen. Thaw tart before reheating. Reheat at work on the base of a sandwich press (do not close the press).

SALMON AND LEEK QUICHES

prep + cook time 1¼ hours (+ refrigeration) **makes** 4
nutritional count per quiche 43.8g total fat (23.7g saturated fat); 2542kJ (607 cal);
21.6g carbohydrate; 31.5g protein; 2.5g fibre

You need four 10cm (4-inch) springform
tins for this recipe.

1 sheet shortcrust pastry
2 small leeks (400g)
50g (1½ ounces) butter
415g (13 ounces) canned red salmon, drained
3 eggs
⅓ cup (80ml) thickened (heavy) cream
½ cup (60g) coarsely grated cheddar cheese

1 Cut pastry into four squares. Roll squares
on lightly floured surface until large enough
to line four 10cm (4-inch) springform tins.
Ease pastry into tins, press into bases and
sides; trim edges. Place tins on oven tray;
refrigerate 20 minutes.
2 Meanwhile, preheat oven to 200°C/400°F.
3 Trim leeks, leaving 5cm (2 inches) green
stem attached. Quarter leeks lengthways;
chop finely.
4 Melt butter in large frying pan over medium
heat. Cook leek, stirring, until starting to
soften; cook, covered, over low heat, about
5 minutes or until soft. Transfer to large bowl.

5 Drain salmon; discard skin and bones.
Flake salmon over leek in bowl.
6 Whisk eggs, cream and cheese in large
jug. Season. Stir through salmon mixture.
7 Cover pastry with baking paper; fill with
dried beans or rice. Bake 10 minutes; remove
beans and paper. Bake pastry cases for a
further 10 minutes.
8 Spoon salmon mixture into pastry cases.
Bake quiches about 25 minutes or until
mixture is golden and set.

notes Cool quiches before packing in
airtight containers. Refrigerate quiches for
up to 2 days, or freeze, wrapped, for about
3 months. Thaw overnight in the fridge. At
work, reheat on the base of a sandwich press
(do not close the press), or on low in the
microwave, however, the pastry won't be as
crisp. If you like, pack a green leafy salad
and dressing, separately, to accompany the
quiche at lunch.

PORK AND FENNEL SAUSAGE ROLLS

prep + cook time 50 minutes (+ cooling) **makes** 8
nutritional count per roll 16.9g total fat (7.6g saturated fat); 1201kJ (287 cal);
18.7g carbohydrate; 14.2g protein; 1.6g fibre

1 tablespoon olive oil
1 medium fennel bulb (300g), trimmed,
   chopped finely
3 cloves garlic, crushed
400g (12½ ounces) minced (ground) pork
2 eggs
½ cup (35g) stale breadcrumbs
¼ cup (30g) grated cheddar cheese
2 tablespoons finely chopped fresh
   flat-leaf parsley
1 teaspoon finely grated lemon rind
2 sheets puff pastry
1 teaspoon fennel seeds
1 teaspoon white sesame seeds

1 Heat oil in large frying pan over medium heat. Cook chopped fennel, stirring, about 10 minutes or until softened. Stir in garlic; cook until fragrant. Cool.

2 Combine fennel mixture, pork, 1 egg, breadcrumbs, cheese, parsley and rind in large bowl; season.

3 Preheat oven to 220°C/425°F. Line two oven trays with baking paper.

4 Cut both pastry sheets into four squares. Place about ½-cup of the pork mixture along one side of square; roll to enclose. Place, seam-side down, on tray. Repeat with remaining pastry and pork mixture.

5 Lightly beat remaining egg. Brush rolls with egg; sprinkle with combined seeds.

6 Bake rolls about 20 minutes or until pastry is golden and filling is cooked through; cool.

notes Cooled rolls can be stored in airtight containers, in the fridge, for up to 2 days. You can also freeze the rolls cooked, or uncooked, before brushing with egg. Uncooked rolls can be baked from frozen. Thaw baked rolls before reheating.
At work, reheat in a toaster oven or on the base of a sandwich press (do not close the press). Rolls may also be gently heated in a microwave, however, the pastry will not be as crisp.

LAMB AND SPINACH SAMOSAS

prep + cook time 1¼ hours (+ cooling) **makes** 24
nutritional count per samosa 12.9g total fat (6.4g saturated fat); 931kJ (222 cal);
18g carbohydrate; 7.8g protein; 1.5g fibre

2 medium potatoes (400g), chopped finely
200g (6½ ounces) finely chopped thawed
   frozen spinach
1 tablespoon vegetable oil
1 medium brown onion (150g), chopped finely
5 cloves garlic, crushed
4cm (1½ inch) piece fresh ginger (20g), grated
500g (1 pound) minced (ground) lamb
½ cup (150g) madras curry simmer sauce
1 tablespoon lemon juice
6 sheets puff pastry
1 egg, beaten lightly

1 Boil, steam or microwave potato until
tender. Drain; cool.
2 Squeeze out excess moisture from spinach.
3 Heat oil in large frying pan over medium
heat; cook onion, garlic and ginger, stirring,
until soft. Add lamb; cook, stirring, over high
heat, until browned. Stir in sauce; simmer,
uncovered, 5 minutes. Stir in potato, spinach
and juice; season to taste. Cool.

4 Preheat oven to 220°C/425°F. Line oven
trays with baking paper.
5 Cut each pastry sheet into four squares.
Place 2 tablespoons lamb mixture in centre
of each pastry square. Brush edges of pastry
with egg. Fold pastry over filling to make
triangles; press edges with a fork to seal.
6 Place triangles on trays; brush with egg.
Bake about 30 minutes or until golden.

notes Choose a mild curry simmer sauce
if making samosas for children. Check the
curry sauce does not contain nuts.
Cool rolls before packing into airtight
containers. Refrigerate rolls for up to 2 days.
You can also freeze the samosas before
brushing with egg, uncooked, or baked.
Uncooked rolls can be baked from frozen.
Thaw baked rolls before reheating. At work,
reheat in a toaster oven or on the base of a
sandwich press (do not close the press). Rolls
may also be gently heated in a microwave,
however, the pastry will not be as crisp. Pack
some yogurt separately to serve with the
samosas, if you like.

SPICY BEEF EMPANADAS

prep + cook time 1¼ hours (+ cooling) **makes** 28
nutritional count per serving 13g total fat (6.5g saturated fat); 917kJ (219 cal);
20.1g carbohydrate; 5.2g protein; 1g fibre

You need an 11cm (4½-inch) round cutter
for this recipe.

2 eggs
1 medium desiree potato (200g),
   chopped finely
2 teaspoons olive oil
1 small brown onion (80g), chopped finely
2 cloves garlic, crushed
250g (8 ounces) minced (ground) beef
½ teaspoon each ground cumin and
   smoked sweet paprika
¼ teaspoon dried chilli flakes, optional
½ cup (125ml) beef stock
2 teaspoons tomato paste
2 tablespoons sultanas
¼ cup (30g) seeded green olives
7 sheets shortcrust pastry

1 Cook one egg in a small saucepan of
boiling water for 7 minutes or until hard
boiled. Drain under cold water. When cool
enough to handle, peel egg.
2 Meanwhile, boil, steam or microwave
potato until tender. Drain; cool.
3 Heat oil in large frying pan over medium
heat; cook onion and garlic, stirring, until
soft. Add beef; cook, stirring, over high
heat, until browned. Stir in spices; cook
until fragrant. Add stock, paste, potato and
sultanas; simmer, uncovered, for about
3 minutes or until sauce thickens.
4 Meanwhile, coarsely chop boiled egg and
olives. Stir into beef mixture; season. Cool.

5 Preheat oven to 200°C/400°F. Line two
large oven trays with baking paper.
6 Using an 11cm (4½-inch) round cutter,
cut 28 rounds from pastry. Drop 1 rounded
tablespoon of beef mixture in centre of each
round; lightly brush edges with water. Fold in
half to enclose filling, pinch edges to seal.
Place empanadas, seam-side up, on trays;
brush edges with remaining lightly beaten
egg. Bake about 30 minutes or until
empanadas are browned lightly.

notes Cool empanadas before packing
in airtight containers; refrigerate for up to
2 days. Empanadas can also be frozen
cooked or uncooked. Uncooked empanadas
can be baked from frozen. Thaw baked
empanadas before reheating.
At work, reheat in a toaster oven or on the
base of a sandwich press (do not close the
press). Rolls may also be gently heated in a
microwave, however, the pastry will not be
as crisp. Pack some chutney or tomato
sauce to serve the empanadas, if you like.

BABA GHANOUSH a roasted eggplant (aubergine) dip or spread. Available ready-made from most supermarkets.

BACON SLICES also known as rashers of bacon, made from pork side, cured and smoked.

BEANS

    broad also known as fava, windsor and horse beans; available dried, fresh, canned and frozen. Fresh and frozen forms should be peeled twice (discarding both the outer long green pod and the beige-green tough inner shell).

    kidney medium-size red or white bean, slightly floury in texture yet sweet in flavour; sold dried or canned.

    mixed usually a combination of kidney, butter and cannellini beans and chickpeas.

BREADCRUMBS, STALE one- or two-day-old bread made into crumbs by blending or processing.

BUTTER use salted or unsalted (sweet) butter; 125g is equal to one stick (4 ounces) of butter. Unsalted butter, often called "sweet" butter, simply has no added salt.

BUTTERMILK originally the term given to the slightly sour liquid left after butter was churned from cream, today it is made similarly to yogurt. Sold alongside all fresh milk products in supermarkets; despite the implication of its name, it is low in fat.

CAPERS the grey-green buds of a warm climate (usually Mediterranean) shrub, sold either dried and salted or pickled in a vinegar brine. Baby capers, those picked early, are very small, fuller-flavoured and more expensive than the full-size ones. Capers, whether packed in brine or in salt, must be rinsed well before using.

CAPSICUM also known as bell pepper or, simply, pepper. Seeds and membranes should be discarded before use.

CELERIAC also known as celery root. A tuberous root with a brown skin and white flesh. It has a soft, velvety flesh that turns creamy when mashed, with a subtle celery-like flavour. Can also be eaten raw.

CHEESE

    cream cheese commonly known as Philadelphia or Philly, a soft cow's-milk cheese. Sold at supermarkets.

    fetta a crumbly goat- or sheep-milk cheese with a salty taste.

    ricotta the name for this soft, white, cow's-milk cheese roughly translates as 'cooked again'. It's made from whey, a by-product of other cheese-making, to which fresh milk and acid are added. Ricotta is a sweet, moist cheese.

CHICKPEAS also called channa, garbanzos or hummus; round, sandy-coloured legume.

CHILLI available in many types and sizes. Use rubber gloves when seeding and chopping fresh chillies as they can burn your skin. Removing seeds and membranes lessens the heat level.

    flakes crushed dried chillies.

    long available both fresh and dried; a generic term used for any moderately hot, long, thin chilli (about 6cm to 8cm long).

CHORIZO a very spicy, deeply smoked sausage of Spanish origin. Made of coarsely ground pork and highly seasoned with garlic and chill; available as both dry-cured and raw.

CIABATTA in Italian, the word means slipper, which is the traditional shape of this popular white bread with a crisp crust.

COCONUT, DESICCATED unsweetened, concentrated, dried, finely shredded coconut.

CORIANDER also known as pak chee, cilantro or chinese parsley; bright-green leafy herb with a pungent flavour. Both the stems and roots of coriander are also used; wash well before using. Also available ground or as seeds; these should not be substituted for fresh coriander as the tastes are completely different.

CORNFLOUR also known as cornstarch; used as a thickening agent. Available as 100% maize (corn) and wheaten cornflour.

CORNICHONS French for gherkin, a very small variety of cucumber.

COUSCOUS a fine, grain-like cereal product made from semolina; a dough of semolina flour and water is sieved then dehydrated to produce minuscule even-sized pellets of couscous; it is rehydrated by steaming, or by the addition of a warm liquid, and swells to 3-4 times its original size.

CREAM we use fresh cream, also known as pouring, single and pure cream, unless otherwise stated.

sour a thick commercially-cultured soured cream with a 35% fat content. Light sour cream has 18.5% fat content.

thickened (heavy) a whipping cream containing a thickener. Fat content 35%.

CUMIN, GROUND a spice also known as zeera or comino; has a spicy, nutty flavour.

EGGS some recipes in this book may call for raw or barely cooked eggs; exercise caution if there is a salmonella problem in your area. The risk is greater for those who are pregnant, elderly or very young, and those with impaired immune systems.

FEFFERONI PEPPERS bottled pickled peppers. They come in mild and hot varieties and are available from many larger supermarkets. They can be substituted with any other type of pickled chilli.

FELAFEL a Middle Eastern dish of spiced mashed chickpeas or other pulses formed into balls and deep-fried.

FENNEL also known as finocchio or anise; eaten raw in salads or braised or fried as a vegetable accompaniment. Also the name given to dried seeds having a licorice flavour.

FLAT-LEAF PARSLEY also known as continental parsley or italian parsley.

FLOUR

plain an all-purpose flour made from wheat.

self-raising plain or wholemeal flour combined with baking powder in the proportion of 1 cup flour to 2 teaspoons baking powder. Also called self-rising flour.

GINGER, FRESH also known as green or root ginger; the thick root of a tropical plant.

GREEK-STYLE YOGURT often made from sheep milk; its thick, smooth consistency is attained by draining off the milk liquids.

HORSERADISH CREAM a commercially prepared creamy paste made of grated horseradish, vinegar, oil and sugar.

KUMARA Polynesian name of orange-fleshed sweet potato often confused with yam.

LEBANESE CUCUMBER short, slender and thin-skinned. Probably the most popular variety because of its tender, edible skin, tiny, yielding seeds, and sweet, fresh taste.

LEEK a member of the onion family, resembles the green onion but is much larger and more subtle and mild in flavour.

MAYONNAISE a rich, creamy dressing made with egg yolks, vegetable oil, mustard and vinegar or lemon juice.

japanese mayonnaise is made using apple cider vinegar or rice vinegar, along with a small amount of mustard and MSG. It is generally richer in taste than western mayonnaise.

MESCLUN mixed baby salad leaves also sold as salad mix or gourmet salad mix; a mixture of assorted young lettuce and other green leaves.

MILK CHOC BITS also known as chocolate chips or chocolate morsels; comes in milk, white and dark chocolate varieties. Contains an emulsifier, so hold their shape in baking and are ideal for decorating.

MILO a chocolate malted sweetened milk drink base.

MIRIN a sweet rice wine used in Japanese cooking; not to be confused with sake.

MUSTARD

dijon a pale brown, fairly mild french mustard.

seeds black, also known as brown mustard seeds, are more pungent than the yellow (or white) seeds used in most prepared mustards.

ONIONS

green also known as scallion or, incorrectly, shallot; an immature onion picked before the bulb has formed, having a long, bright-green edible stalk.

red also known as spanish, red spanish or bermuda onion; a sweet-flavoured, large, purple-red onion.

PAPRIKA a ground dried sweet red capsicum (bell pepper); there are many grades and types available, including sweet, hot, mild and smoked.

POLENTA also known as cornmeal; a flour-like cereal made of ground corn (maize). Also the name of the dish made from it.

POTATOES

desiree oval, smooth and pink-skinned, with a waxy yellow flesh; good in salads, boiled and roasted.

kipfler (fingerling) small, finger-shaped, knobby potato with a nutty flavour; great baked and in salads.

PRESERVED LEMONS a North African specialty; lemons are quartered and preserved in salt and lemon juice. To use, remove and discard pulp, squeeze juice from rind, rinse rind well, then use. Sold in jars or in bulk by delicatessens; once opened, store preserved lemon in the refrigerator.

PROSCIUTTO a thinly-sliced dry-cured Italian ham, comes in two varieties: prosciutto crudo (raw) and prosciutto cotto (cooked).

QUINOA pronounced keen-wa. The seed of a leafy plant similar to spinach. Its cooking qualities are similar to rice, and its delicate, slightly nutty taste and chewy texture make it a good partner for rich or spicy foods. You can buy it in most health-food stores and some delicatessens; keep quinoa sealed in a glass jar under refrigeration because, like nuts and nut oils, it spoils easily.

ROCKET also known as arugula, rugula and rucola; a peppery-tasting green leaf that can be used similarly to baby spinach leaves.

SAUCES

madras curry a hot curry sauce. The commercial version may contain coriander, cumin, pepper, turmeric, chilli, garlic, ginger, vinegar and oil.

soy made from fermented soya beans. Several variations are available in most supermarkets and Asian food stores. We use a mild Japanese variety in our recipes; possibly the best table soy and the one to choose if you only want one variety.

SHALLOT also called french shallots, golden shallots or eschalots; small, elongated brown-skinned members of the onion family. Grows in tight clusters similar to garlic.

SNOW PEAS also called mange tout ('eat all').

SOBA NOODLES thin spaghetti-like pale brown noodle from Japan made from buckwheat and varying proportions of wheat flour.

SPINACH also known as english spinach and, incorrectly, silver beet. Its thick, soft oval leaves and green stems are both edible. Baby spinach is also available – it is more tender.

SUGAR

brown, light an extremely soft, fine granulated sugar retaining molasses for its characteristic colour and flavour.

caster also known as superfine or finely granulated table sugar.

icing sugar mixture also known as confectioners' sugar or powdered sugar; granulated sugar crushed together with a small amount of added cornflour (about 3%).

SULTANAS dried grapes, also known as golden raisins.

TAHINI a sesame seed paste available from Middle-Eastern food stores.

TOMATOES

cherry also known as tiny tim or tom thumb tomatoes, small and round.

egg also called plum or roma, these are the smallish, oval-shaped tomatoes much used in Italian cooking.

grape are about the size of a grape; they can be oblong, pear or grape-shaped.

VANILLA BEAN dried long, thin pod from a tropical golden orchid; the tiny black seeds inside the bean are used to impart a luscious vanilla flavour.

extract made by extracting the flavour from the vanilla bean pod; the pods are soaked, usually in alcohol, to capture the authentic flavour.

VINEGAR

red wine based on fermented red wine.

rice a colourless vinegar made from fermented rice and flavoured with sugar and salt. Also known as seasoned rice vinegar.

WATERCRESS also known as winter rocket, is a slightly peppery, dark-green leaf. Highly perishable, so use as soon as possible after purchase.

WEET-BIX a flaky wheat-based breakfast biscuit; oven-roasted whole wheat grains, sugar, salt and barley malt extract.

ZUCCHINI also known as courgette; small green, yellow or white vegetable belonging to the squash family.

CONVERSION CHART

MEASURES

One Australian metric measuring cup holds approximately 250ml, one Australian metric tablespoon holds 20ml, one Australian metric teaspoon holds 5ml.

The difference between one country's measuring cups and another's is within a 2- or 3-teaspoon variance, and will not affect your cooking results. North America, New Zealand and the United Kingdom use a 15ml tablespoon. All cup and spoon measurements are level. The most accurate way of measuring dry ingredients is to weigh them. When measuring liquids, use a clear glass or plastic jug with metric markings.

We use large eggs with an average weight of 60g.

DRY MEASURES

METRIC	IMPERIAL
15g	½oz
30g	1oz
60g	2oz
90g	3oz
125g	4oz (¼lb)
155g	5oz
185g	6oz
220g	7oz
250g	8oz (½lb)
280g	9oz
315g	10oz
345g	11oz
375g	12oz (¾lb)
410g	13oz
440g	14oz
470g	15oz
500g	16oz (1lb)
750g	24oz (1½lb)
1kg	32oz (2lb)

LIQUID MEASURES

METRIC	IMPERIAL
30ml	1 fluid oz
60ml	2 fluid oz
100ml	3 fluid oz
125ml	4 fluid oz
150ml	5 fluid oz
190ml	6 fluid oz
250ml	8 fluid oz
300ml	10 fluid oz
500ml	16 fluid oz
600ml	20 fluid oz
1000ml (1 litre)	1¾ pints

LENGTH MEASURES

METRIC	IMPERIAL
3mm	⅛in
6mm	¼in
1cm	½in
2cm	¾in
2.5cm	1in
5cm	2in
6cm	2½in
8cm	3in
10cm	4in
13cm	5in
15cm	6in
18cm	7in
20cm	8in
23cm	9in
25cm	10in
28cm	11in
30cm	12in (1ft)

OVEN TEMPERATURES

These oven temperatures are only a guide for conventional ovens. For fan-forced ovens, check the manufacturer's manual.

	°C (CELSIUS)	°F (FAHRENHEIT)
Very slow	120	250
Slow	150	275-300
Moderately slow	160	325
Moderate	180	350-375
Moderately hot	200	400
Hot	220	425-450
Very hot	240	475

The imperial measurements used in these recipes are approximate only. Measurements for cake pans are approximate only. Using same-shaped cake pans of a similar size should not affect the outcome of your baking. We measure the inside top of the cake pan to determine sizes.

Published in 2013 by ACP Books, Sydney

ACP Books are published by ACP Magazines Limited,
a division of Nine Entertainment Co.

54 Park St, Sydney
GPO Box 4088, Sydney, NSW 2001.

phone (+61)2 9282 8618; fax (+61)2 9126 3702

acpbooks@acpmagazines.com.au; www.acpbooks.com.au

ACP Books

Publishing director, ACP Magazines – Gerry Reynolds

Publisher – Sally Wright

Editorial & food director – Pamela Clark

Creative director – Hieu Chi Nguyen

Sales & rights director – Brian Cearnes

Published and Distributed in the United Kingdom by Octopus Publishing Group

Endeavour House

189 Shaftesbury Avenue

London WC2H 8JY

United Kingdom

phone (+44)(0)207 632 5400; fax (+44)(0)207 632 5405

info@octopus-publishing.co.uk;

www.octopusbooks.co.uk

Printed by Toppan Printing Co, China

International foreign language rights · Brian Cearnes, ACP Books bcearnes@acpmagazines.com.au

A catalogue record for this book is available from the British Library.

ISBN 978-1-74245-389-7